A gift to Tom & Athena Holtey from Ann McCaren, Peggy's nurse.
A gift to Jean Hurley from Tom & Athena

Peggy Chun

"BOO"

"Sieyo the second"

# The Watercolor Cat

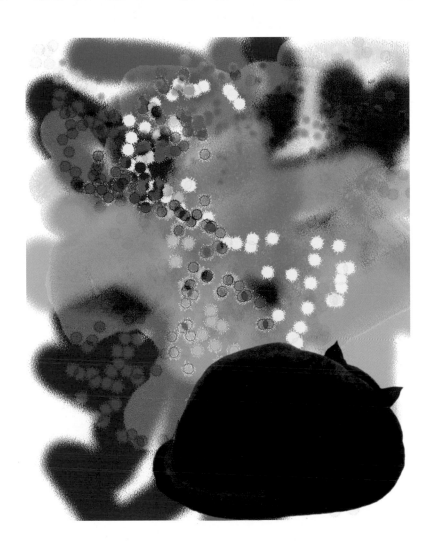

## Art by Peggy Chun

## Story by Shelly Mecum

Mutual Publishing

## Dedication

For Elroy, Eric, Kimi, Indy, Sawyer,
Jason, Jenifer, Jade, Cian, Shelly, Roger,
Bug, "Pegs Legs" and our Beloved Boo
—Peggy

For Peggy, Christine, Wally, Roger,
Eden-Lee, Hélène, Susan, Val, Suzanne,
Mardie, John, Joey, Bill, Mom and
Dad—*You know who you are.*

—Shelly

Art copyright © 2007 by Peggy Chun
Text copyright © 2007 by Michelle Mecum

ISBN-10: 1-56647-838-3
ISBN-13: 978-1-56647-838-0

First Printing, October 2007
Second Printing, February 2008

Printed in Taiwan

Library of Congress Cataloging-in-Publication Data

Mecum, Shelly.
  Watercolor cat / the art by Peggy Chun ; text by Shelly
Mecum.
    p. cm.
  ISBN 1-56647-838-3 (hardcover : alk. paper)
 1. Chun, Peggy--Juvenile literature. 2. Painters with
disabilities--Hawaii--Juvenile literature. I. Chun, Peggy. II.
Title.
ND1839.C564M43 2007
759.13--dc22
[B]
                                                2007020954

Mutual Publishing, LLC
1215 Center Street, Suite 210
Honolulu, Hawaii 96816
Ph: (808) 732-1709 / Fax: (808) 734-4094
email: info@mutualpublishing.com
www.mutualpublishing.com

"If you hear a voice within you say

'*you cannot paint,*'

then

by all means **PAINT**

and that voice will be silenced."

—Vincent Van Gogh

Oops!

**Boo Rider**

I hate to be vain. But I believe I am the only cat in the world with an a.k.a. Also Known As. An a.k.a. is only given to the very, very, very famous or the very, very, very mischievous. My friends and family know me by my real name, Sara. However, in the world of art, I am also known as Boo.

Banana Patch Heaven

I live in a plantation style house, on a small island in Hawai'i, with a very, very, very famous artist named Peggy Chun. I love Peggy and she loves me. Peggy "luvluvluvs me soooo much" that she has painted me over and…

*over and
over again,*

**Boo and Plumeria**

**Boo and Melon**

**Boo at Leisure**

in watercolor paintings—hence the need
for my a.k.a. name of BOO.

**Boo and Spider**

If everyone knew my real name, well, I would never be able to sit quietly and ponder the doings of spiders.

I would have to hide myself from my throngs of fans.

Boo in Bowl

Peggy Chun ©'97

Boo in Ti Patch

So Peggy protects my identity and I am able to wander freely around my island in peace, without anyone recognizing me and making a big fuss.

Boo and Laua'e

I came to Peggy as a small kitten. She had just begun her
career as a watercolor artist. I would shyly peek at
her through the leaves of the Laua'e fern, as she painted.
I sensed that she was sad about something.

11

One night, as I sat on her lap listening, Peggy cried and cried
and told me about the loss of her mother, Sarah, and
her twin sister, Bobbie. They had both died from ALS, a fatal
disease that runs in Peggy's family.

**Nabe's Shadow**

I could only soothe her with my purring. Now I understood the secret sorrow behind her eyes. I made a promise to Peggy that night. I promised never to leave her—and so began our friendship.

**The Road to Hana**

Our life together took on a sweet rhythm. I liked to nap
in the mornings. When I finally stretched and softly padded
my way up the stairs to her studio, I would find Peggy in
a whirlwind of painting.

Faces of the Flowers

Colors and water were splashed on the paper
creating lush tropical scenes. Simply watching her
paint made me purr deep inside.

Spirit of the Paddles

*And she painted…*

Hauʻoli Ia Hanau

*and painted…*

**Maka Makai**

*and painted…*

Temptation

Mele Pua

A Gift of Lei

*and painted and painted and painted.*

19

**Udder Nonsense**

Here's a secret about my friend Peggy. She won't
mind if I share this with you. Sometimes Peggy painted
the most whimsically when she was feeling the blues.
She cheered herself up through her paintings. Peggy laughed
aloud to see all her cows float off the canvas.

Day off from the Dairy

Peggy's undersea world off the coast of Lahaina on the island of Maui included the usual subjects— colorful coral, tropical fish, smiling dolphins, and … snorkeling cows? I guess if they can float they can swim.

**Zoo Rain**

*And she painted…*

**Little Orchestra on the Prairie**

*and painted…*

**Switchbacks**

*and painted…*

Hoofin' It

Pua'a Aloha

Pig Tales

*and painted and painted and painted.*

Peggy was asked to paint a portrait of Mother Marianne Cope. Mother Marianne came to Hawai'i in 1888 to care for the victims of Hansen's Disease at Kalaupapa, on the island of Moloka'i.

Mother Marianne

Peggy so rarely painted people. Simply painting hands can be difficult for an artist.  But she couldn't let fear stop her from trying. So Peggy picked up her paintbrush and painted.

Peggy was troubled by odd twitches in her legs. Sadly, she knew what this meant. She had ALS—the same disease that took the life of her mother and twin sister, Bobbie.

Na Hana Lei o Punahou

Peggy told only a handful of friends. Her friends knew what to do. They named themselves "Peg's Legs." Their plan was simple. Two friends would be at her side, every hour of the day or night. Peggy would never be left alone.

They did simple things for her. They washed the dishes, swept the floors, and loaded the washing machine. They took her out for picnics in the park.

Passion Moon

Inspired by their love, Peggy painted...

Lily Love

Moon River

*and painted and painted.*

Boo and Bug

One morning, after my nap, I sleepily padded my way into Peggy's bedroom. She was laughing with a couple of "Peg's Legs."

"Good morning, Sara. Go see my latest painting! I painted that with my left hand!"

I ran to her studio to see. I couldn't believe it. It was me! She painted me with her left hand!

I ran back to Peg's room. She beamed at me and said. "I
love this hand! I love this hand!" And Peggy playfully kissed
her left hand and arm all the way to her shoulder.

Her right hand lay motionless on her lap. She
could no longer move it.

**Red Ti**

*She painted and…*

Laua'e

Na Kalo

*painted and painted with her left hand.*

Pali Pines

Peggy's left hand grew weaker each day. But more troubling for Peggy was her breathing. The muscles of her lungs were growing weak. Peggy could not get enough air.  She went to the hospital.

The doctors decided she needed to go on a ventilator. This is a machine that would help Peggy breathe for the rest of her life. Peggy was very afraid. The night before surgery, Peggy cheered herself up by painting. This would be Peggy's last left-handed painting. No one knew this at the time.

Indy's Eyes

I must have looked worried when Peggy came home. Peggy asked me to join her in bed. There were tubes in her throat that helped her to breathe. Her left and her right arms lay motionless now. But her spirit was strong in her eyes.

"Sara, everything that happens to us, happens to us for the right reason. Let's wait to worry," she said.

Then we brought her to her studio so she could paint with a special brush held by her teeth. And she painted…

Lakeside Flowers

and painted

and painted with
her teeth.

Koke'e Garden

Merci Bouquet

Trade Showers

Ko'olau Cove

Boo in Contemplation

Slowly her jaw muscles weakened. She could not hold the brush with her teeth. Peggy could no longer paint! Then her vocal cord muscles lost strength. Her voice grew quieter than a whisper.

Peggy could no longer speak!  That night, I talked to God.

Boo Moon

"God? Can you hear me? It's me, Sara. Peggy is in trouble. She cannot move. She cannot paint. She cannot speak. Please, help her. Peggy is the bravest of the brave and she's afraid. I love her, God. She needs a miracle. Please, say 'Yes' and help her."

Indiana demonstrates how her grandmother talks with her eyes.

And God said, "Yes!"

The first miracle: Peggy can spell with her eyes!

Since only her eyes can move, a friend creates a special spelling board. Now Peggy can spell messages to family and friends. The very first thing she spells is "I love you" to her granddaughter Indy, the smallest "Peg's Leg" in the room.

And she talks and talks and talks with her eyes!

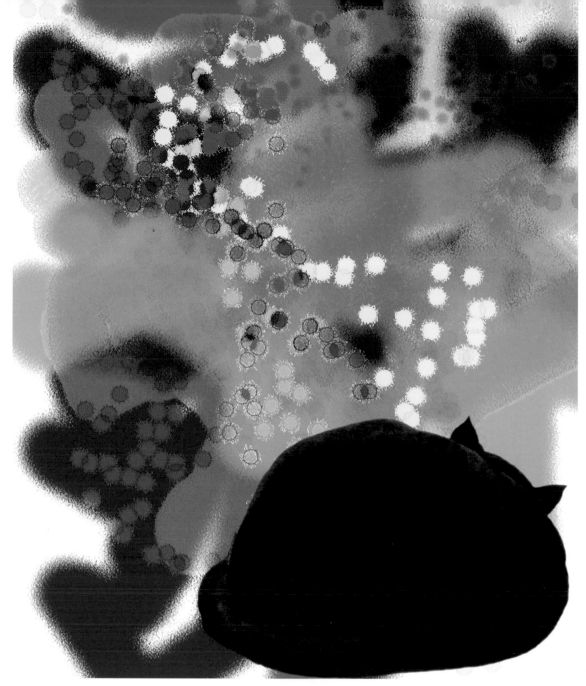

**Eye Heart You**

The second miracle: Peggy can paint with her eyes!

A new computer system, named ERICA, allows Peggy
to simply gaze at the computer screen and type and talk and
digitally paint.

And she paints and paints and paints with her eyes!

**Celebration in the Banana Patch**

Peggy's family, friends, and scientists gather together to witness the third miracle. I curl up on Peggy's shoulder as she lies still and silent in her bed.

Navajo Nightfall

The scientists gently place sensors on her forehead. Peggy will control the palette of colors either by silently singing a campfire song—Under the Bamboo Tree—or wordlessly picturing fluffy, white clouds.

And she paints and paints and paints with her thoughts!

Ka Pili me ka Makuahine (Madonna and Child)

"After all," Peggy says,
"you don't paint with your hands;
you paint with your heart."

44

And she is still painting
and painting
and painting.

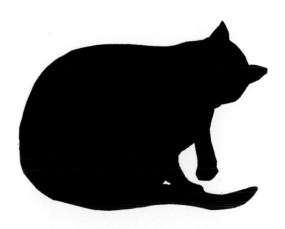

Peek-a-Boo!

# A Statement from the Artist

George F. Lee / *Honolulu Star-Bulletin*

To All of You Creative Friends:

In January 1990, two seemingly unrelated events took place: I sold my first painting; within a week, an abandoned furry black kitten was given to me. Seventeen years later Boo still remains my muse, among all the other gracious cat idiosyncrasies of which she is capable.

What a bond we have! This little love sponge has never left my side. She has always been a part of the creative activity in my house and studio, even painting her own originals for my upcoming show—unwillingly and unwittingly, of course.

Boo keeps me company, sleeping on my right shoulder whenever opportunity affords. You see, I am now fully paralyzed, and now I'm still, Boo is thrilled to have me always available as a sleeping place! Before I became paralyzed, I was in a constant whir of activity. My lap was never free long enough for a satisfying catnap, so Boo compensated by sleeping on every painting, wet or dry! I'm sure Boo's hair is embedded in paintings hanging around the world! If I moved her off to the side of the table, I would see a paw slowly inching its way to the edge of the paper. Meeting her comfort level simply meant that she would be part of everything I created.

I tell you this about Boo because she will tell my story. Boo has seen it all from the beginning of my art career, and what a journey it has been! I am here to tell you how afraid I've always been; that overcoming fear is the only way to grow. Any of you who paint, write, perform or create in any form have great courage! I was fortunate enough in the beginning to not only have my own late twin sister's artistic spirit guiding me, but also that familiar dilemma most artists face—no money! Fear was a driving force— which would be worse, fear of criticism, or not paying the rent? I could never have taken on some of the challenges without this pressure to survive.

Art opens the mind and provides a joy that can't be verbalized.  The four simple steps for creating art I learned from one of my most respected teachers, Catherine Chang Liu:

HOW TO MAKE A PAINTING…

1. Get Started
2. Don't Stop and Compare
3. Don't Judge Yourself
4. Keep Going

My life has been one adventure after another because of the choices I've made. So go for life at its fullest. I'm so glad I did, fear and all! Now as I lie in my bed typing with my eyes I feel a soft warm purring friend at my side, one paw touching my hand.

Let me now tell you who makes all this ability to continue painting possible. It's the love of my son Eric and his loving wife Kimi—a rare spirit. Also our 100 or more Peg's Legs who keep me fully functional as a complete human being. And all the donations and other sources of support.

The only security is courage!

As I look at the last past years all the while planning and working on several on-going projects, I'm reminded of another favorite from an old friend: Life is full of memories and as those memories are worthwhile so is life worth the living.

I'm now living life second by second which means I'm living the cat's philosophy which I daresay sounds like the Creator's advice. Seize the second!

I'm proud to be among you!

Thank you,

Peggy Chun